C000180744

Women of faith
what they teach us

NICK FAWCETT

kevin
mayhew

First published in 2002 by
KEVIN MAYHEW LTD
Buxhall, Stowmarket, Suffolk IP14 3BW
Email: info@kevinmayhewltd.com

9 8 7 6 5 4 3 2 1 0

ISBN 1 84003 922 1
Catalogue No 1500514

Cover design by Angela Selfe
Edited by Katherine Laidler
Typesetting by Louise Selfe
Printed and bound in Great Britain

Contents

To Rob and Diane Allen
and all the family
with thanks for your constant friendship across the years

Acknowledgements

The publishers wish to express their gratitude to Toc H, 1 Forest Close, Wendover, Aylesbury, Bucks, HP22 6BT, for the prayer 'Loving Father, you have made all people' (adapted).

Bible quotations are taken from the New Revised Standard Version of the Bible, copyright © 1989 by the Division of Christian Education of the National Council of the Churches of Christ in the USA. Used by permission. All rights reserved.

Introduction

'It's a man's world', so the saying goes, and looking through a selection of encyclopaedias as I prepared the quiz questions for this book brought home to me as never before just how shockingly true that has been. Whether in the sphere of politics, religion, science or the arts, for every woman who has gone down in posterity there must be a hundred men. Is that because men are more gifted or able? Of course not! The simple fact is that across the centuries and throughout the world women have suffered the most appalling discrimination, and, in many places, still do. Tragically, one of the last bastions of sexism in our own society is the Church – the very last place you might expect to find it. Didn't the Apostle Paul himself, despite his frequent chauvinistic language, maintain that there is no longer male or female, all being one in Christ? Yet, in almost every Christian denomination I know of, the representation of women in leadership is grossly disproportionate to their overall number, and the majority are still expected to occupy subordinate roles.

If there is still discrimination today, however, it was all the more rampant in the days of the Old and New Testaments, which makes those women whose stories are told in Scripture all the more remarkable. In this study course, I have focused on six women in particular: Ruth, Esther, Mary (the sister of Martha), the woman who touched Jesus' cloak, the woman at the well, and Lydia. I could equally have chosen others: Anna, the prophetess, who waited so patiently to see the promised Messiah; the woman who washed Jesus' feet in a spontaneous outpouring of love; Mary Magdalene, who followed Jesus as faithfully as any of the Apostles, if not more so; Dorcas, who spent her days using her gift in practical service; and many more besides. The six I have chosen, however, represent a cross-section of women of faith from both the Old and New Testaments, their stories offering a distinctive challenge while simul-taneously highlighting, or at least touching on, issues of prejudice. Ruth speaks to us as the voice of the outsider; Esther intercedes on behalf of a racial minority; while the incident of the woman at the well raises issues of religious intolerance. The story of Martha and Mary can be seen as questioning the role traditionally assigned to women; and underlying the story of the woman who touched Jesus' cloak is the fact that, because of her condition, she would have faced years of discrimination through being considered ritually unclean. Even the story of Lydia contains overtones of prejudice, only this time it is prejudice directed against those who profess faith in Christ.

This book is not a token gesture to political correctness. When I sat down to write it, I intended to explore on a very simple level the stories of six biblical women, only it didn't work out that way, for as I studied each one it became clear to me that their experiences said something about the prejudices that from time immemorial have divided people from one another. In a world where women at almost every level of society all too often fail to receive due recognition and where numerous other divides – race, age, creed and sexuality – continue to scar our society, I felt I could not ignore such issues. Legislation may have brought us a long way in combating discrimination, but deep-rooted attitudes and precon- ceptions persist. Indeed, despite my best efforts, my own language may very well inadvertently reflect stereotypical images, so ingrained have some of these become in our culture.

All this is not to say that the importance of the women covered in this book lies solely in their making themselves heard in a male- dominated society. Each provides a distinctive example of faith in her own right. Read this book, then, on two levels, exploring first the challenges these women bring but considering also the wider issues their stories raise. If you think such issues do not apply to you, perhaps you need to consider them most of all!

Nick Fawcett

Leader's notes

I suggest using the material in this book as follows:

- Each session begins with a traditional prayer, followed by a short paragraph introducing the overall theme. It is worth reading this aloud, to set the scene for the session.

- After this I have included 'Activity' sessions, designed to break the ice and to encourage informal reflection on the theme of the study. Allow ten minutes or so for these, but do not allow them to dominate the session.

- Next comes a Bible passage (my own paraphrase unless otherwise stated). This should be read aloud, and then time given for group members to quietly ponder its meaning.

- Ideally, group members need to have read the 'Comment' section before the meeting, in which case you will need to have circulated booklets in advance of the first session. Alternatively, extend the period of quiet after the reading so that participants can read this section at their own pace.

- The 'Summary' section highlights the key points of the Comment. The leader should read this aloud before inviting people's thoughts on the subject so far.

- Allow discussion to develop, and introduce as appropriate the questions provided in the Discussion section. It may be appropriate at this point to bring in the passage suggested for further reading, though you may prefer to leave this, as I have done, to round off the theme nearer the end.

- Pause for prayer, using the prayer provided, a prayer of your own, or a time of quiet/open prayer.

- After allowing ample time for discussion, read the meditation to draw people's thoughts together. They are taken from my publications *The Unfolding Story* and *No Ordinary Man* (books 1 and 2).

- Briefly outline the suggestions for action. Invite any further ideas from among the group. From the second week onwards, you might also give people the opportunity to share how they applied the suggestions from the previous week.

• Finally, end the meeting in prayer, using either the prayer provided or your own.

Prayer

Gracious God,
    you have told us that in Christ there is neither Jew nor Greek,
    slave nor free,
    male nor female.
You tell us that you value us for what we are,
    and in the Scriptures you show that to be true.
In a world of prejudice and discrimination,
    you called people from all walks of life,
    all strands of society;
    each having a place in your kingdom
    and a contribution to make towards it.
We think especially of the women you called –
    women who, despite the odds stacked against them
    in a male-dominated society,
    demonstrated a level of faith and commitment
    that few of us ever aspire to.
Teach us, through their example,
    to see beyond the artificial barriers we create,
    to be open to all,
    and to respect all.
So, in unity with all your people, may we work for your kingdom,
    bringing it closer here on earth,
    through Jesus Christ our Lord.
Amen.

First week

Ruth: Voice of the outsider

Opening prayer

Loving Father,
   you have made all people in your likeness,
   and love all whom you have made.
Let not the world separate itself from you
   by building barriers of race and colour.
As your Son was born of a Hebrew mother,
   yet rejoiced in the faith of a Syrian woman
   and a Roman soldier,
   as he welcomed the Greeks who sought after him,
   and had his cross carried by a man from Africa,
   so teach all people to regard the members of all races
   as fellow heirs of your kingdom,
   through the same, Jesus Christ our Lord.
Amen.

A Toc H prayer (adapted)

Introduction

The book of Ruth is something of an oddity in the context of the Old Testament. Not only does a woman take centre stage, but she is also, of all people, a Moabite rather than a Jew! Here is a story expressly written with the purpose of raising hackles, its clear aim to challenge the preconceptions of its readers. Think again, it says; look beyond race, religion, sex and culture, or risk losing sight of the God you claim to worship. A fascinating irony of the story is that Ruth's great-grandson was none other than David, one of the most celebrated kings of Israel (see Ruth 4:17-22). Clearly 'race' and 'racial purity' were unimportant to God. A more tragic irony is that few people have suffered more than Jews from racial hatred, the Holocaust a sobering warning to us all of where prejudice can finally lead.

Issues of prejudice are never far from the surface throughout this endearing tale. In an apparently simple story of everyday life and human relationships, God is at work, present where we might least expect to find him – in a young refugee from the pagan land of Moab. On one level, Ruth's story offers an example of selfless devotion and friendship at its highest level; look deeper and we catch a glimpse of the God whose sovereign purpose embraces all.

Activity

Quiz (see page 66).

Reading: Ruth 1:8-17

But Naomi said to her two daughters-in-law, 'Go back each of you to your mother's house. May the Lord deal kindly with you, as you have dealt with the dead and with me. The Lord grant that you may find security, each of you in the house of your husband.' Then she kissed them, and they wept aloud. They said to her, 'No, we will return with you to your people.' But Naomi said, 'Turn back, my daughters, why will you go with me? Do I still have sons in my womb that they may become your husbands? Turn back, my daughters, go your way, for I am too old to have a husband. Even if I thought there was hope for me, even if I should have a husband tonight and bear sons, would you then wait until they were grown? Would you then refrain from marrying? No, my daughters, it has been far more bitter for me than for you, because the hand of the Lord has turned against me.' Then they wept aloud again. Orpah kissed her mother-in-law, but Ruth clung to her. So she said, 'See, your sister-in-law has gone back to her people and to her gods; return after your sister-in-law.' But Ruth said, 'Do not press me to leave you or to turn back from following you! Where you go, I will go; where you lodge, I will lodge; your people shall be my people, and your God my God. Where you die, I will die – there will I be buried. May the Lord do thus and so to me, and more as well, if even death parts me from you!' (*NRSV*)

Comment

In the week that I began writing this session, three news items caught my attention. One concerned a highly ranked Asian police officer, falsely accused of spreading racist hate mail, who endured two years suspended from duty before his name was cleared. Another involved a woman who learned that a man had been offered a position in the firm she worked for, doing exactly the same job but for significantly more money. The third highlighted the continuing prevalence of ageism in Britain today. Sadly, such stories are not rare. Despite all attempts to change attitudes within society, many people still find themselves 'outsiders': women in a man's world, coloured people in a white world, and the aged in a young people's world are just three examples among many.

If that is true, though, today, it was all the more so in the time of Ruth. As a woman, a widow and a foreigner, she wouldn't have had much going for her in the eyes of most Jews at that time, and her prospects in a male-dominated society, generally suspicious of outsiders and hostile towards foreigners, would have seemed bleak indeed. Unsurprisingly, then, her mother Naomi soon had second thoughts about taking her two daughters-in-law back to Judah, deciding their chances would be better among their own families in Moab. 'Go back,' she said, 'each of you to your mother's house. May the Lord deal kindly with you, as you have dealt with the dead and with me' (Ruth 1:8, *NRSV*). Sensible advice, you would have thought, and one of the two clearly agreed. Orpah, after a brief protest, set off as bidden, but with Ruth it was different.

'Do not press me to leave you or to turn back from following you! Where you go, I will go; where you lodge, I will lodge; your people shall be my people, and your God my God. Where you die, I will die – there will I be buried. May the Lord do thus and so to me, and more as well, if even death parts me from you' (1:16-17, *NRSV*). It is a truly unforgettable promise. Though she was under no moral obligation to stay with Naomi, she pledged undying commitment, and as if to prove the point, the moment she arrived in Israel Ruth set busily to work in order to provide for herself and her mother-in-law 'without resting even for a moment' (Ruth 2:7b). Her dedication was soon noted, not least by her mother's kinsman Boaz. 'All that you have done for your mother-in-law since the death of your husband has been fully told me,' he said, 'how you left your father and mother and your native land and came to a people that you did not know before. May the Lord reward you for your deeds, and may you have a full reward from the Lord, the God of Israel, under whose wings you have come for refuge!' (Ruth 2:11, *NRSV*).

Here, then, in Ruth, is an example of devotion far beyond the call of duty, and on that level alone her story has much to teach us concerning commitment to friends, fellowship and family, but to the Jew it said much more. The key point is that Ruth was an outsider, according to the Jewish Law a Gentile, and therefore a second-class citizen compared with God's chosen people. Yet here she was not receiving but giving, not displaying faithlessness but a level of commitment that put most of them to shame. Like the gospel incidents of the Syrophoenician woman and the centurion who came to Jesus for help, and like the parable of the good Samaritan, this is a story recorded expressly to challenge the reader, reminding us that God's love and purpose extend beyond artificial divides, embracing all. Not only does he value every individual for what they are, but he can speak through each of them too. No person, no culture, no creed has a monopoly on truth – we may often find God where we least expect him.

Are we ready to listen and learn from outsiders, those beyond our immediate circle, of family, friends, work, church, society, country, colour or religion? Are we ready to be stretched, our comfortable preconceptions undermined, our prejudices challenged? Are we ready to consider new ideas, different points of view and fresh insights? In the book of Ruth we glimpse a willingness to listen to the voice of the outsider, recognising it as the voice of God. Are we willing to do the same?

Summary

- Prejudice and discrimination is still an inescapable fact today, despite many attempts to combat it.
- As a woman, a widow and a Gentile, Ruth would be a social and religious outsider in Israel. Yet, despite her mother-in-law Naomi's encouragement to return to the land of her birth, she insisted on staying by her side, come what may.
- Ruth exhibited a degree of loyalty and commitment such as few in Israel could attain to. Her story was recorded with the express purpose of challenging narrow and parochial outlooks. It posed a direct challenge to restrictive interpretations of the Jewish Law and the promises of God.
- Are we ready in turn to listen to the voice of the outsider? Are we prepared to have our preconceptions challenged and to recognise that God is able to speak through anyone and everyone?

Discussion

- Declarations of loyalty are easy to make but harder to live up to. How dedicated are you to your friends and family? How many could count on you in their hour of need?
- The book of Ruth was written to challenge the assumptions and prejudices prevalent in Israel at the time. Are there hidden prejudices in our own lives that this story challenges in turn? How often are we guilty of jumping to conclusions about people based on colour, creed, culture or other such characteristics?
- In what ways have you been challenged or inspired by those we term outsiders? Who, for you, are outsiders in society today?

15

Prayer

Loving God,
    we talk about all people having a place in your kingdom,
    but we do not always live as though we believe it.
We try not to pigeonhole people according to the colour of their skin,
    their religion, age or gender,
    yet we have preconceived opinions about what is acceptable
    and unacceptable,
    and we write off anyone who does not conform to our ideas.
We see differences as a threat rather than a gift,
    the prejudices within us running deep,
    poisoning our very soul.
Teach us to look at people with your eyes,
    seeing the good and the bad,
    the lovely and the unlovely,
    the strengths and the weaknesses,
    yet seeing above all our common humanity.
Through Jesus Christ our Lord.
Amen.

Meditation of Ruth

Was I making a mistake staying with her like that?
My sister thought so, plain enough;
    Naomi too, mother-in-law or not.
And I could see why,
    for I was a Moabite, not a Jew,
    belonging, so they thought, with my own people,
    my own family,
    instead of a distant town in a foreign land.
What were my prospects there, you have to say?
What hope of finding a new husband,
    starting a new home,
    building a new life?

Precious little, there was no point denying it –
    I would be a stranger with no place in their history,
    their faith or their customs.
So when she told us to turn back,
    I knew why she said it,
    her only concern for our welfare,
    her thoughts all for us and none for her.
Quite simply, she was exhausted, mentally and spiritually –
    life had dished out one heartbreak too many –
    and though she tried to mask the sorrow with a smile,
    I knew she'd given up,
    ready now to suffer whatever fate might throw at her.
But for us it could be different –
    that's what she hoped anyway –
    just because *her* future seemed grim
    why should *ours* be too?
So yes, like my sister Orpah I could have left in good conscience,
    gone back to the place of my birth.
There'd be a welcome there of sorts,
    and no reason to feel guilty –
    simply doing what was best for all.
Yet when I looked at her standing there,
    so alone,
    so helpless,
    I couldn't walk away,
    not after all we'd shared together.
There were too many memories,
    moments which bound us inseparably together –
    triumphs and tragedies, pleasure and pain –
    each uniting us in a way formal ties could never begin to.
So I stayed, hard though she tried to dissuade me;
    I pledged my love,
    my loyalty,
    come what may.
It looked foolish, you're quite right,
    the wild impulse of a headstrong youngster,

17

but, you see, she wasn't simply a mother-in-law to me,
she was a friend,
the one I'd turned to so often in time of need –
and this time she needed me.
I had a choice, in theory anyway,
but when it came to it there was no question,
none at all.
There was just one answer I could make,
one response which would do.
Could you have acted differently in my place?
I hope not.

Further reading: Galatians 3:28

There cannot now be either Jew or Greek, slave or free, male or female, for you are all one in Christ.

Suggestions for action

Examine yourself honestly for vestiges of prejudice within your life. Resolve to learn more about those concerning whom such prejudice may lurk.

Closing prayer

Living God,
    help us to open our lives to you
    by opening them first to others,
    through Jesus Christ our Lord.
Amen.

Second week

Esther: Voice for the persecuted

Opening prayer

Lord, I know you created me
    for a special purpose,
    to serve you in a unique way.
You have given me a gift, and talents,
    a certain something no one else has.
Help me to be a valuable link
    in the chain of humanity.
Help me to find peace and meaning
    in what I do,
    knowing that no one else can be me.
Amen.

Author unknown

Introduction

'Cometh the hour, cometh the man' – or at least so the old saying tells us. Is it true? Well, it may be, yet few proverbs more clearly illustrate how firmly gender is ingrained in our language and culture. Today we look at someone about whom it could be said 'Cometh the hour, cometh the woman'! Not only does her example call us to rethink our assumptions, but in her readiness to seize the moment God gave her and to make the most of her opportunity, Esther demonstrated faith and courage that most of us can only dream of, her story not about sexual but racial prejudice and an early attempt at systematic genocide. Her courageous plea on behalf of her people asks us whether we are prepared to identify with the oppressed, exploited and outcasts of this world.

The unsuspecting reader may be fooled by the almost complete absence of references to God throughout Esther's story. You might almost think it is simply a tale of good triumphing over evil – the stuff of legends and fairy stories. Yet to this day Esther is revered within Judaism not simply as a model of courage but above all as an example of faith. Hers was an example of selfless devotion, freely putting her welfare second to others, never mind the consequences. We should not be deceived by the absence of religious terminology from the narrative. Esther's faith and service was as real as that offered by any other. She may not have interpreted her heroic gesture in this way, but that serves only to highlight the importance of what she has to teach us. Faith and life went hand in hand for her, each indissolubly linked, the one a natural outworking of the other. Can the same be said of us?

Activity

Quiz (see page 66).

Reading: Esther 3:8-10; 4:1, 5, 9-16

Then Haman said to King Ahasuerus, 'There is a certain people scattered and separated among the peoples in all the provinces of your kingdom; their laws are different from those of every other people, and they do not keep the king's laws, so that it is not appropriate for the king to tolerate them. If it pleases the king, let a decree be issued for their destruction, and I will pay ten thousand talents of silver into the hands of those who have charge of the king's business, so that they may put it into the king's treasuries.' So the king took his signet ring from his hand and gave it to Haman son of Hammedatha the Agagite, the enemy of the Jews. . . . When Mordecai learned all that had been done, Mordecai tore his clothes and put on sackcloth and ashes, and went through the city, wailing with a loud and bitter cry . . . Then Esther called for Hathach, one of the king's eunuchs, who had been appointed to attend her, and ordered him to go to Mordecai to learn what was happening and why. . . . Hathach went and told Esther what Mordecai had said. Then Esther spoke to Hathach and gave him a message for Mordecai, saying, 'All the king's servants and the people of the king's provinces know that if any man or woman goes to the king inside the inner court without being called, there is but one law – all alike are to be put to death. Only if the king holds out the golden sceptre to someone, may that person live. I myself have not been called to come in to the king for thirty days.' When they told Mordecai what Esther had said, Mordecai told them to reply to Esther, 'Do not think that in the king's palace you will escape any more than all the other Jews. For if you keep silence at such a time as this, relief and deliverance will rise for the Jews from another quarter, but you and your father's family will perish. Who knows? Perhaps you have come to royal dignity for just such a time as this.' Then Esther said in reply to Mordecai, 'Go, gather all the Jews to be found in Susa, and hold a fast on my behalf, and neither eat nor drink for three days, night or day. I and my maids will also fast as you do. After that I will go to the king, though it is against the law; and if I perish, I perish.' (*NRSV*)

Comment

Have you ever written to your Member of Parliament or local newspaper about an issue that concerns you? If you're like me, there will have been many times when you felt you ought to but did nothing about it except perhaps sign the odd petition or circular letter provided by organisations such as Christian Aid. All kinds of reasons might explain our failure to act. We may, for example, have had second thoughts about the matter, being able to see arguments for and against, and therefore deciding we could not favour one position against the other. We may have felt out of our depth, unqualified to pass judgement when we were not in full possession of the facts. We may have been hesitant about getting involved in moral or ethical issues, afraid that through doing so we might somehow reinforce stereotypical images of Christianity. In short, there may be numerous valid reasons for keeping our thoughts to ourselves, yet I suspect that more often than not the real reason we say nothing is that we either can't be bothered to put ourselves out or are worried that making a stand may potentially count against us. We fear being labelled an activist or radical, or getting sucked into something deeper than we want to go, and so instead of speaking out or putting pen to paper we keep our counsel, suppressing the voice of conscience.

In a sense, that was true initially of Esther. A Jew by birth, she found favour with Ahasuerus, king of Persia, to the extent that he wanted to take her as one of his wives and make her queen. It was an opportunity too good to miss, but her cousin Mordecai advised her that in order to grasp it she needed to conceal her Jewish roots, for were it to become known that she was a member of a subject people characterised by a radically different creed and culture it could have jeopardised all. So it was that she concealed her identity without any qualms, her nationality a matter for herself and her own conscience, but then came a drastic change in circumstances that was to force her to think again. A young man, Haman, was promoted to high office, second only to the king himself, and all subjects were ordered to bow in homage before him. For Mordecai, as for his fellow Jews, such homage was tantamount to idolatry, so he refused the command, and as a result the infuriated Haman plotted to destroy not just Mordecai but every Jew within Persia. The king's authority was duly secured, and throughout the empire Jews waited in terror for the inevitable slaughter to begin.

Could anyone help? Was there anything that could be done to avert disaster? There was just one possibility, and it revolved exclusively around Esther. As wife to the king, she alone might be in a position to influence him and rescue her people. Yet it was by no means a simple matter, for no wife of the king, not even a queen, was permitted to approach him unbidden. As Esther told Mordecai's messenger, when he came to her begging for help, 'All the king's servants and the people of the king's provinces know that if any man or woman goes to the king inside the inner court without being called, there is but one law – all alike are to be put to death. Only if the king holds out the golden sceptre to someone, may that person live. I myself have not been called to come into the king for thirty days' (Esther 4:11, NRSV). We can scarcely begin to imagine the agonies of indecision Esther must have gone through after that meeting, wrestling with inner fears on the one hand and her conscience on the other. She could keep quiet and perhaps save her neck at the cost of her people, or she could plead their cause and risk the very real prospect of death. It must have seemed an impossible dilemma, but then came another message from Mordecai, and with it a challenge that was to throw new light on the situation, helping her to see it not so much as a quandary as a God-given opportunity. 'Who knows? Perhaps you have come to royal dignity for just such a time as this' (Esther 4:14b). Here was a suggestion that brought a new factor into the equation, enabling her to view it from an altogether different perspective. Perhaps God had put her where she was for a reason. Perhaps catching the king's eye and becoming his wife hadn't just been a quirk of fate but part of God's purpose, leading up to this moment. Whatever else, here was her opportunity to put her circumstances to good use.

There were still no guarantees, of course; indeed, nothing outwardly had changed. The difference was not in the situation but in Esther. Inspired by the possibility that God could use her, she suddenly found undreamed-of courage. 'I will go to the king,' she said, 'though it is against the law; and if I perish, I perish' (Esther 4:16b, NRSV). The time had come to speak out, to fling aside her reservations and toss caution to the wind. That is not to say she didn't make herself as alluring as possible before approaching her husband – if God had his part to play she also had hers – but she knew ultimately that her fate was in divine hands, not her own.

None of us is likely to face a predicament anything like Esther experienced, nor to be in any such elevated position, but there may nonetheless be a time and a place in which God wants to use us. It may be among our colleagues at work or the friends we mix with socially. It may be through words or deeds, through offering practical support or through speaking out, whether on behalf of others or against evil. It may be through writing to our MP or contacting a local councillor, through joining a campaign or signing a petition, through sharing in a March of Witness or participating in a protest rally. It may, above all, be through standing up for the oppressed, identifying with them and being ready to make sacrifices on their behalf. Whatever it is, there are times when God wants to use us and our situation towards the furtherance of his kingdom and fulfilment of his will. We can tell ourselves we're not needed, that his purpose will prevail with or without our help, that we're better off minding our own business rather than interfering, but the trouble is we may be wrong. As with Esther, it may be that God is depending on us, we those he is able to work through at a particular moment, if only we are willing to respond. To return to the proverb we started with, 'Cometh the hour – what about us?'

Summary

- We sometimes feel we ought to make a stand about something, yet remain silent for fear of the consequences. We prefer a quiet life to getting involved.
- Esther initially kept quiet about her nationality rather than jeopardise the prospect of becoming queen. When her people were faced with extermination, however, she was the only one in a position to intercede on their behalf.
- Esther was faced by a dilemma, having to choose between her own safety and identifying with her people. She came to see this, however, not as a quandary but a God-given moment. This was her opportunity to use her situation and circumstances in the service of God.
- We too at certain moments in our lives may find ourselves in a position to act in the furtherance of God's will. Ordinary situations may be transformed into God-given opportunities to participate in the fulfilment of his purpose.

- Are we ready to identify with the oppressed and rejected in society? Are we ready to grasp the moment, when God calls?

Discussion

- Esther was willing to put her life in jeopardy for the sake of her people. How much would you be willing to sacrifice in the cause of others?
- Are there moments you can think of when your being in a certain place at a certain time allowed God to use you in a special way?
- What factors prevent you from taking risks in the cause of Christ?
- What sort of people do we need to identify with today? About which issues do you think Christians should be making a stand?

Prayer

Living God,
   for us all there come opportunities to serve you;
      to use our gifts, position or circumstances to further your purpose.
You do not force us to respond,
   but you invite us to share in making your love real on earth.
We can offer ourselves freely,
   or hold back, afraid of the cost,
      reluctant to let go.
Forgive us that all too often we choose the latter;
   that through our failure to give *to* you
      we deny our claim to live *for* you.
Inspire us through the example of those who have risked everything
   in the cause of your kingdom,
      and help us, remembering the one who sacrificed all,
         to give the little you ask from us.
In his name we pray.
Amen.

Meditation of Esther

Could I honestly make a difference?
It seemed hard to believe,
    the very idea preposterous,
    but I had to try,
    for surely anything in the circumstances was worth a go?
My people were under threat,
    not just the odd one or two, but every one of them,
    facing the prospect of wholesale slaughter.
I couldn't just stand by and let them face their doom,
    however ineffectual my efforts might be,
    for we were inseparably bound,
    the same culture,
    the same faith,
    the same God.
If anyone could help them, I could.
Not that there were any guarantees, I knew that –
    the fact that I was his wife counted for nothing.
He was the king,
    ruler of a mighty empire,
    the difference between life and death dependent on his whim;
    and I was but one of many,
    each vying for his favour,
    each waiting for his call.
I'd pleased him once –
    could I do so again?
It wasn't just *my* future that rested on the answer,
    it was my nation's,
    the fate of us all hanging by a thread.
Yet I had no qualms,
    no second thoughts;
    incredible though it seemed,
    I realised God had put me there for such a time as that.
It was my chance to serve him,
    to do my bit for his kingdom,

and I couldn't afford to waste it.
So I went –
    ignoring tradition,
    flouting every rule in the book,
    I entered his chamber and stood before him.
Was he surprised?
I was too terrified to notice,
    but to my amazement he listened –
    attention personified –
    and when I'd finished he gave the order,
    not for *our* death,
    but the death of those who would have seen us killed.
We were safe,
    free to walk the streets with heads held high,
    and together we gave thanks to God.
But do you know what happened next?
I'm afraid so – they made me a celebrity,
    much to my embarrassment.
No, I'm not being modest, despite what some may think.
I took a risk, it's true,
    and yes, it could have cost me my life,
    but no more than if I'd closed my eyes and done nothing,
    my fate irrevocably tied to my people's.
I did what I could, that's all,
    what God would have asked of anyone –
    the rest was down to him.

Further reading: 2 Corinthians 12:15
I will most gladly spend and be spent for you. (*NRSV*)

Suggestions for action

If there is a situation where you recognise God is able to use you, or where you feel it is right to make a public stand, stop dithering and act.

Closing prayer

Lord Jesus Christ,
    you faced up to evil,
    even though it cost you your life.
Give me wisdom to know when I must stand up for my convictions,
    and stand out for others,
    and then give me courage to stand firm,
    for your name's sake.
Amen.

Third week

Mary, sister of Martha: Voice of the heart

Opening prayer

O heavenly Father, in whom I live and move
 and have my being,
I humbly pray that you will guide me by your Holy Spirit,
 that in all the cares and occupations of my daily life
 I may never forget you,
 but remember that I am always walking in your sight.
Amen.

Author unknown

Introduction

We live today at breakneck speed, rushing here, there and every-
where, yet forever chasing our tails. Despite having labour-saving
gadgets our grandparents could only have dreamed of, we are part
of a society ravaged by exhaustion and burn-out as we attempt
to cram yet more activity into our already overcrowded lives.
The material rewards are many, yet spiritually most of us are
hopelessly impoverished.

We need sometimes to pause and ask ourselves where we are
going and why. We need to consider the deeper things of life and
to reflect on what actually matters most. Unless we pause to think
now, we may reach the end of our days only to discover that we
have frittered our lives away on much that is ultimately empty
and meaningless trivia.

Activity
Screwball Scramble® (see page 67).

Reading: Luke 10:38-42
As they continued on their way, he entered a certain village, where a woman called Martha welcomed him into her home. She had a sister called Mary, who sat at the Lord's feet, listening to his words. Martha, however, was preoccupied with her many tasks, so she came to him and asked, 'Lord, doesn't it matter to you that my sister has left me to do all the work by myself? Tell her, then, to lend a hand.' But the Lord answered her, 'Martha, Martha, you are fretting and distracted by many things; only one thing is really important. Mary has chosen that more important thing, and it will not be taken away from her.'

Comment
It had been a rush; a truly frenetic day spent rushing around like a scalded cat as I attempted to get a hundred and one jobs done at once, but at last the end was in sight. Just one more job to do – an important letter that needed to catch the evening post – and then I could finally relax and take a well-earned breather. Frantically, I scrawled my signature across the bottom of the page, dashed off to find a stamp, scribbled the recipient's name and address on the envelope, sealed it and raced to the post box, just as the postman was pulling up in his van to empty it. Success! Only it wasn't, for when I got home and slumped wearily into a chair, the first thing I spotted was my letter lying on the table. In my haste, I'd posted an empty envelope!

I expect we can all recall moments when we've made similar mistakes. Perhaps we cooked a meal and forgot to salt the vegetables, or went shopping and forgot to take any money, or set off on a journey and forgot to fill up first with petrol. When we're rushed off our feet, preoccupied with concerns or simply feeling frazzled, such clangers are easy to make. All of which will cause us to have more than a little sympathy for Martha's situation in the incident related above. Not that she made the sort of hapless blunders I have spoken of. As far as we know, she was every inch the efficient and competent hostess, someone who knew exactly what she was about. An important guest had come to dine, and her overriding concern was to look after his needs, to ensure Jesus was as much at home and as well fed as possible, and I've no doubt she succeeded admirably in that aim. Never mind the fact there'd been no time to prepare in advance – the meal she rustled up that day would, I'm sure, have been fit for a prince. Yet beneath the unflustered façade, her mind was in turmoil, all kinds of thoughts rushing through her head. Look at the state of the house! If only she'd known in advance that Jesus might pass by. What *would* he think of her? What was he thinking *now*? Had he enough to drink? How was she going to keep lunch warm? Was there enough to go round? Had she dusted behind the chairs? Look at all the washing-up! And all the time Mary was sitting there, moon-eyed, listening to Jesus as if she hadn't a care in the world. Had she no thought for her poor harassed sister? How could she just sit there without lifting a finger to help, and, equally galling, how could Jesus let her do so? It just didn't seem fair that one person should toil away in the kitchen while another was given all the attention, and suddenly her sense of injustice, resentment and anger boiled over. 'Lord, doesn't it matter to you that my sister has left me to do all the work by myself? Tell her then to lend a hand' (Luke 10:40b).

It's hard not to feel sorry for Martha, isn't it? We've probably all been in a situation similar enough to empathise with how she was feeling and to share something of her pique. Surely Mary could have done something to ease the load. If she'd only helped a little, it would have saved Martha running herself into the ground, and then the two of them could have sat down to listen to Jesus together. But would that actually have happened? If Mary *had* got up and done her bit, would Martha then have made time for

Jesus? Would she ever have been satisfied that everything else had been seen to so that she could give him her undivided attention? As I read it, the implication of this story is that she wouldn't; not because she didn't want to or didn't value Jesus, but because her priorities were muddled, her very concern not to forget something leading her to forget what mattered most. She failed to understand that whatever she might offer to Jesus, he had more to offer her; that he had come not simply to receive but to give, not to be fed but to feed. Above all, he wanted to meet her needs rather than have Martha meet his, and though he was no doubt grateful for her attentions, he was saddened equally by her inattentiveness to his message.

Mary stands in complete contrast. She may well have had a lazy streak in her – who can say? For all we know, she may have been glad of an excuse to take a few minutes' break, especially if, as seems possible, Martha was always on at her to do this or that. Yet such thinking wasn't what motivated Mary here. Rather, she realised that this was a special moment, a time so precious that other concerns paled into insignificance beside it. Whatever else needed doing, it could wait; this was her chance to listen to Jesus first-hand, to hear his words to her, to seek his guidance and advice, and she wasn't going to waste it, even if it meant a rollicking afterwards. So it is that Mary emerges from this story with a word of commendation, while Martha, for all her good intentions, ends up with a firm if gentle reprimand: 'Martha, Martha, you are fretting and distracted by many things; only one thing is really important. Mary has chosen that more important thing, and it will not be taken away from her' (Luke 10:41).

It is a wonderfully human story, in which both sides of the argument are plain to see, and perhaps that's why it appeals to so many, but, of course, it is not recorded simply for entertainment. Luke recounts this incident because he believes it presents an important challenge that Jesus wants us to reflect on in turn: namely, do we make sufficient time for the things that matter? On one level, this relates to the things of God, or, in other words, our spiritual well-being. Don't let your life become so cluttered, says

Jesus, so busy, that God is squeezed out of it. Don't be so preoccupied with day-to-day pressures, responsibilities and concerns that you neglect the spiritual dimension to life. Such things may well be important, but they are not finally what count the most. Make time for worship, prayer and the study of God's word. Make time for seeking his will and discerning his guidance, for listening, reflecting and responding. Make time for him and you will find a proper time for everything.

If that, though, is the chief message of this story, we can, I think, push it a little further, beyond what we might term our 'devotional life' to life in general. How often do we, like Martha, brood, fret and worry unnecessarily? How often do we become steamed up over things that, in the final analysis, are neither here nor there? All too easily, we spend our time rushing around, feeling that we should always be doing something, or chasing after illusory happiness. We are part of a world in which many, perhaps ourselves included, have lost the ability to stop and stare, and in which more and more people find themselves sucked ever deeper into a spiral of anxiety and stress from which they find it impossible to escape. To find time to sort our priorities and focus on what really matters is not easy, but it is essential. Maybe we need more time for our children or partner, perhaps for a friend, neighbour or colleague, or perhaps for ourselves. Perhaps we need to pause and take stock, to consider where we're going and why. Perhaps we need to adapt our lifestyle, modify our ambitions or simply count our blessings. Unless we find time to do it, we will not find the contentment we crave.

Just what it was that Jesus said to Mary as she sat listening at his feet we are not told, but perhaps it was along the lines of the Sermon on the Mount: 'Do not fret about life, about the things you will eat or drink, or about how you will clothe your body. Do not brood about tomorrow, for tomorrow will bring its own anxieties. Today's problems are quite enough for today' (Matthew 6:25, 34). Or perhaps it was more like those equally lovely words: 'Come to me, all you that are weary and are carrying heavy burdens, and I will give you rest. Take my yoke on you and learn from me, for I am tender and lowly in heart and you will find rest for your souls – for my yoke is easy, and my burden is light' (Matthew 11:28-30). Or perhaps, again, it was more akin to the promise he made to the Apostles in the Upper Room: 'Peace I leave with you. I give you my peace' (John 14:27). This is what Mary found that day Jesus came to dine. This is what Martha was still searching for, even though she had not begun to realise it. This is what Jesus offers us: a peace that passes understanding, quietness of spirit, rest for our souls. Whatever else you may forget, don't forget that!

Summary

- Sometimes, in the frenetic bustle of life, we can overlook simple but important things.
- So it was with Martha. She was so busy attending to Jesus' needs, making sure she didn't forget anything, that she forgot what mattered most of all: the reason Jesus had come and the gift he had to offer.
- Mary realised that everything else was secondary to what Jesus was able to give. She put aside other concerns in order to make time for him.
- We too need to make time for Jesus and for the things of God. Neglect our spiritual well-being, push prayer, reflection and devotions to one side, and the whole of life will suffer.
- In life as a whole, we need to reflect on what is important and what is incidental. Too easily, we are drawn into a rat race that ultimately leads us nowhere. We need to make time now for the things that really count.
- The promises of Jesus challenge us concerning our priorities, and remind us of the special gifts he alone can offer. They are gifts we cannot afford to overlook.

Discussion

- Do you succeed in making time for quiet reflection, or are such moments crowded out by the demands and concerns of daily life?
- What is the hardest thing in being still and quiet? Have you any suggestions as to what might help overcome such problems?
- Apart from our faith, what things in life matter most to us? What things tend to be squeezed out? What do we wish we'd made more time for when we had the chance?

Prayer

Lord Jesus Christ,
    you have promised to all who love you
    a peace that passes all understanding.
Forgive us that so often we fail to make that our own.
We rush about, our minds preoccupied by many things,
    filling our days with frantic activity,
    cramming ever more into every moment,
    our lives dominated by a sense of the unforgiving minute.
We strive and hanker after that which is finally unimportant,
    unable to satisfy,
    brooding and worrying over problems that we cannot change,
    magnifying little things out of all proportion.
Forgive us that for all our busyness
    we so often forget the one thing needful,
    the one thing that really matters –
    the knowledge of your love.
Help us to live each day,
    each moment,
    with that foremost in our minds,
    and so may we find your peace,
    the rest for our souls that you have promised.
In your name we ask it.
Amen.

Meditation of Mary

I felt sorry for Martha, I really did –
    she was doing her best after all.
Someone had to see to the hospitality,
    make sure the dinner was all right,
    wash up after us;
    and, to be honest, I felt I wasn't pulling my weight.
I could see she was growing harassed,
    despite the smile she kept on her face.
She didn't say anything, but she didn't need to,
    I could tell by the way she looked that she was angry –
    and with good reason.
It was selfish of me,
    unforgivable,
    but I couldn't help myself.
He was so fascinating,
    so easy to listen to,
    so genuine.
It was as though every word he spoke was for me,
    answering the questions I'd never dared to ask,
    meeting the needs I never even knew existed,
    giving me the sense of purpose I had so long yearned to find.
How could I get up to wash dishes –
    interrupt him to offer another drink?
It would have been sacrilege.
I knew I might never have another chance like that again,
    and so, shame on me, I sat back and let Martha get on with it.
I wasn't surprised when she finally complained,
    but I was by the answer Jesus gave her.
I expected him to back her up, give me a ticking off –
    after all, fair's fair.
But instead he praised me
    and rebuked her!
He spoke gently, of course,
    almost tenderly,

yet it was a rebuke for all that.
I don't know how *she* felt
    but *I* could have died of embarrassment.
It was my fault, you see,
    me who effectively earned her that reprimand,
    and I expected her to be furious afterwards –
    I know I would have been.
Yet, funnily enough, she wasn't.
She was very quiet for a time,
    very thoughtful,
    and then she told me not to look so guilty,
    for Jesus had been right.
He'd made her face herself for the first time,
    and she realised now that she couldn't go on running for ever,
    couldn't go on hoping being busy
    would disguise the emptiness inside.
She'd been made to stop and ask herself what life was all about,
    and in Jesus she had begun to find the answers.
She's still the efficient hostess, of course –
    always will be.
And me?
I'm just as ready to find an excuse for laziness, given half the chance!
But we've changed, both of us,
    grown closer,
    found inner contentment,
    become more at peace with ourselves,
    because through meeting Jesus
    we've each discovered what really counts,
    the one thing we really need.

Further reading: Isaiah 30:15

Thus said the Lord God, the Holy One of Israel: Come back, be at peace, and you will be safe; your strength lies in quietness and being still.

Suggestions for action

Resolve to make time this week, somewhere, somehow, simply to be quiet before God, not rushing through a Bible reading or squeezing in a prayer, but simply being still and allowing him to speak. Resolve also to make time for yourself and your loved ones.

Closing prayer

Lord of all,
    go with us now into the turmoil of life,
    with all its noise and confusion,
    its demands and responsibilities,
    and may your peace rest with us there,
    this day and for evermore.
Through Jesus Christ our Lord.
Amen.

Fourth week

The woman who touched
_____ *Jesus' cloak: Voice for the sick* _____

Opening prayer

O Lord, this is my desire:
    to walk along the path of life
    that you have appointed for me,
    in steadfastness of faith,
    in lowliness of heart,
    in gentleness of love.
Let not the cares or duties of this life
    press upon me too heavily,
    but lighten my burden
    that I may follow your way in quietness,
    filled with thankfulness for your mercy.
Amen.

Maria Hare

Introduction

'Let's just give it one more go.' How often have we used words like those? Perhaps we're unable to start the car in the morning, perhaps wrestling with a crossword puzzle, perhaps trying to get our head round a difficulty, perhaps struggling with an awkward DIY project – whatever it is, we get to the point when we're almost ready to give up; almost, but not quite, for there's a stubborn streak in most of us that impels us to have one final attempt. Astonishingly, that last effort often seems to work, coming up trumps when all else has failed. Why is that? It may simply be that we keep on trying until we succeed, so that, by definition, our final stab proves decisive. Equally, repeated disappointments may cause us to explore new avenues and try anything as a last resort.

Which of those two possibilities do you think most fits the story of the woman who touched the cloak of Jesus in her search for healing? On the one hand, we could argue that she tried all the orthodox channels before turning to Jesus, and perhaps several unorthodox channels too – who knows? On the other, she seemed quite convinced that one touch of Jesus would be sufficient to make her well, yet she may well have approached each of the physicians she'd consulted previously with the same confidence. Again, who can say? The fact is, we do not know for sure what was going through her head. What we do know is that she was willing to give Jesus a go, and that willingness was to prove enough.

Activity

Quiz (see page 67).

Reading: Mark 5:25-34

A woman, who for twelve years had endured a persistent haemor-rhage and who had suffered greatly at the hands of numerous physicians, spending everything she had in the process yet getting worse as a result rather than better, heard about Jesus. Pushing through the crowd, she touched his robe, saying, 'If I can only touch his clothes, I will be healed.' Straightaway, her bleeding stopped and she knew within herself that she had been made well. Jesus, however, instantly aware that power had been drawn from him, spun round in the mêlée and asked, 'Who touched my clothes?' His disciples responded, 'How can you ask "Who touched me?" when you can see for yourself this multitude swarming round you?' Despite this, he persisted in looking for the one who had touched him. Knowing what had taken place within her, the woman fearfully crept forward and prostrated herself in trepidation before him and blurted out the truth. He said to her, 'Daughter, your faith has made you whole; go in peace, and be healed of your illness.'

Comment

What do Thomas Hardy, Vincent Van Gogh, and Franz Schubert have in common with the woman who touched Jesus' cloak? The answer is that all of them were prepared to try and try again, despite disappointment and adversity. Thomas Hardy is revered as one of the greatest English-speaking novelists, and yet when he sent his first book to a publisher he was strongly advised to forget writing and concentrate on his work as an architect. Van Gogh is probably one of the best-known artists in history, yet during his lifetime he sold only one painting! Franz Schubert composed a vast and hugely respected repertoire of music, yet he achieved little recognition in his own day. Each, however, despite the setbacks they faced, kept on trying, refusing to give up.

So it was for the woman who touched Jesus' cloak, a woman who had endured a persistent haemorrhage for twelve long years, hoping against hope that one day she might find a cure. Just imagine what she must have gone through. At the start, no doubt, she was full of optimism, believing as she made her way to a physician that it would only be a matter of time – a few days, weeks or months at most – before her problems were over. Even when that failed, she must have been quietly confident that a second opinion might provide a solution and restore her to health, but then, slowly, the frustrations must have mounted up, as one fruitless journey led to another, a succession of empty promises and unrealised expectations. How would you have felt in her situation? Would you have kept on trying or given up? Would you have battled on or curled up in a corner and accepted your fate? This unfortunate woman could so easily have concluded there was nothing that could be done, no point in trying any longer.

After all she'd been through – not just the emotional and physical trauma but also the financial cost – perhaps it was time to make the best of a bad job, to draw a line under her efforts and face facts. For all we know, she'd done just that, long since throwing in the towel, but then suddenly she sees this crowd and hears people crying out for healing. It is Jesus, the one everyone is talking about, a man who, word has it, is able to transform even the most hopeless of situations, bringing new hope, health and life where all seems lost. Suddenly her hopes are reborn, the past forgotten, her only concern to reach out and touch him. Undaunted by the crowds thronging around him, each as desperate as she to get close; undaunted by the fact that under Jewish law she is ritually unclean and therefore prohibited from touching Jesus; undaunted by the possibility of yet another wasted effort; somehow she jostles her way through the crowd, until at last she is able to reach out and touch his clothes. It is a mere touch, the most fleeting of encounters, yet somehow it is enough for her to know deep within that she has been made well.

So what do we make of this astonishing incident? I have to say that it raises for me as many questions as it answers. Why did God allow the woman to suffer for so long before responding to her need? Why did she become ill in the first place? And why are so many never physically healed, despite their prayers and trust in God? As always when it comes to faith, we are in the realm of mystery. We do not understand and, in this life, we probably never will. Yet there can be no denying the importance to health, as with life and faith in general, of never giving up, never losing hope and never forgetting what God is able to do in Christ. When an individual loses the will to live or surrenders in the battle against disease, there can only be one result. Conversely, numerous people have defied all expectations, recovering from illnesses and injuries that had seemed certain to end in death. We cannot divorce body, mind and spirit, for each is dependent on the other. As the old saying has it, 'Where's there's life, there's hope', and when that life is nurtured and sustained by faith in Christ, there is no telling what might be done, however hopeless things may seem.

The same holds in many other areas of life. When you come up against difficulties to which there seems no solution, never give up. When hopes are dashed and dreams thwarted, never despair. When faith is tested and teeters on the brink, never lose hope. When you find yourself giving in yet again to temptation, all your good intentions yet again coming to nothing, never lose heart. If we are to attempt anything and achieve anything, we need to keep on plugging away even when our efforts seem to get us nowhere, to keep on striving even when life doesn't go to plan. Is that how we respond? Do we shrug disappointment aside and persevere, or do we give up and count our losses? Do we, like the unnamed woman of this story, have the faith and courage to bounce back from disappointments and try again? There's no guarantee that persistence will be rewarded, that perseverance will always win the day. On the contrary, there will be times when we have to recognise a goal is beyond us, or that God is saying no, or that for reasons we do not understand certain things cannot be. This woman's story reminds us, however, that it is only when we are prepared to keep on trying, come what may, that there is any hope of the impossible becoming possible.

We could well leave the woman's story there, feeling that we have considered the key issues raised, but I'm not sure we have, for one detail is all-important. Why was it that the woman touched only the hem of his cloak, and why was she so afraid when Jesus realised what had happened? The reason, of course, is that according to the Jewish law her haemorrhage made her ritually unclean, and by touching Jesus she made him unclean in turn. This was just the tip of the iceberg. That so-called uncleanness would have precluded this woman from entering the temple or synagogue, and equally from touching friends and colleagues – in other words, it affected every part of her life, her relationship both with God and with others. This woman found healing but, as we have already observed, many do not. What of such people today – sufferers from AIDS, the terminally ill, those who are physically disabled or otherwise impaired, the mentally disturbed and those with other emotional disorders – how far are they precluded from living a normal life? We may not be talking here about prejudice in the usual sense, but in what ways are these people treated differently, denied access to the things we take for granted, or denied the opportunity to participate fully in society? Such questions, of course, raise complex issues for which there are no easy solutions, but they are questions concerning ordinary people like you and me who have a right to live life as fully as possible. Whether or not they find physical, mental or emotional healing, God considers every one of them a whole person and wants each to enjoy an inner sense of wholeness. As Christians and a society we have a responsibility to do what we can to prevent incapacity denying any individual's humanity.

Summary

- In common with many illustrious figures from history, the woman who touched the cloak of Jesus showed a determination not to give up.

- Despite repeated disappointments, when she heard of Jesus she resolved to reach out and touch him.

- In terms of healing, the incident raises as many questions as it answers. While there are undoubtedly astonishing incidents of healing, the prayers of many are not answered as they would wish.

- Notwithstanding such questions, perseverance and faith are unquestionably important in combating illness and disease. When hope is lost, the battle is all but over.

- In life, generally, it is important not to give up but to believe that God is able to do what seems impossible.

- At a deeper level, this incident highlights the situation of those who are unable to participate fully in society due to illness or disability. God regards each one of us as a whole person, irrespective of our state of health. As a society, we have a responsibility to ensure that everyone is able to live life as fully as possible.

Discussion

- What place do you see for Christian healing alongside traditional medicine and alternative therapies? How do you make sense of those who are not healed?

- Have there been times in life when you've felt like giving up on something, only to find persistence rewarded? What were these? Where did you find strength to continue?

- In what ways are people prevented from living life to the full through illness or incapacity? What can be done to overcome this? How far is your church open to those with disabilities? How far are *you* open?

Prayer

Loving Lord,
    you are always looking to respond to our needs,
    constantly reaching out to touch our lives with your love,
    yet all too often we fail to seek the help you long to give us.
We trust in our own strength,
    we try this, that and everything else,
    and we only remember you when we reach the end of our tether
    and there is no one left to turn to.
Forgive us for relegating you to the periphery of life
    rather than putting you at the centre.
Forgive us for treating you as a last resort
    instead of a first recourse.
Teach us to bring our needs to you,
    knowing that though you may not always respond
    as we want you to,
    you will always respond in love,
    providing for our needs,
    granting us peace
    and bringing us the wholeness that you alone can give.
In your name we ask it.
Amen.

Meditation of the woman who touched Jesus' cloak

I was sick –
    sick of body,
    sick of mind,
    sick of spirit –
    fed up with having my hopes raised only to be dashed again,
    fed up with everything.
I'd suffered for so long,
    my strength failing,
    my fears multiplying,
    and I was ready to give up,
    to say goodbye to it all,
    to curl up in some dark corner and let life slip away.
But then suddenly I saw him, just a few yards in front of me,
    the man they were all talking about –
    Jesus of Nazareth,
    prophet,
    teacher,
    worker of miracles –
    and it took only one glance to convince me
    he was the answer to my prayers.
Yes, I was desperate, admittedly,
    ready to believe anything, clutch at any straw,
    but there was more to it than that,
    for I could see immediately that this man was unique,
    everything about him proclaiming his love for others.
So I pushed my way through the crowds
    and I reached out and touched him,
    just the faintest of contacts, that's all,
    yet immediately I felt whole again,
    a knowledge deep within that I was well.
But before I had time to celebrate I froze in horror,
    for he stopped,
    and turned,
    and looked around curiously,

eyes sweeping over the crowd.
Goodness knows how he'd felt my touch amongst so many,
    but he had,
    and I realised then the awfulness of what I'd done,
    breaking every commandment in the book
    by touching him in my condition.
I waited for the rebuke,
    the explosion of anger that would shatter my illusions,
    yet it never came;
    just that one simple question:
    'Who touched me?'
There was no escape.
Though I longed to melt away into the crowd,
    I knew there could be no deceiving this man,
    so I shambled forward and blurted out the whole story,
    pleading for forgiveness,
    begging him to make allowances.
I still feared the worst,
    but finally I dared to meet his eyes,
    and there he was,
    gently returning my gaze,
    a look of love and understanding that I shall never forget.
'Daughter,' he said, 'your faith has made you well.
    'Go in peace, and be healed of your disease.'
It was true – the affliction had gone –
    but there was more than that,
    much, much more.
I'd found new meaning, new hope, new purpose,
    strength that I'd never known before,
    peace that I'd never imagined possible.
He sensed my need that day before I even expressed it,
    responding instinctively to my silent plea,
    and I'm whole now –
    whole in body, mind and spirit –
    ready for whatever life might bring,
    ready for anything!

Further reading: John 10:10

I have come to you so that you shall have life, and have it to the full.

Suggestions for action

Give something this week to a charity dedicated to improving the quality of life of those suffering from illness or disability.

Closing prayer

Lord Jesus Christ,
    before I do anything else
    help me always to turn to you,
    and so may I know your hand upon me,
    this and every day.
Amen.

Fifth week

_ The woman of Samaria: Voice of the despised _

Opening prayer

Here I am, Lord – body, heart and soul.
Grant that, with your love,
  I may be big enough to reach the world,
  and small enough to be at one with you.
Amen.

Mother Teresa

Introduction

From a chance encounter to a searching examination, from a passing exchange to a challenging dialogue – that is what we see in the story of the woman by the well. Approached by a stranger asking for a drink, before she knows it she finds herself confronted by uncomfortable home truths, drawn into something far deeper and far more challenging than she had ever anticipated. Meeting with Christ is like that, or at least it should be. It involves a journey of self-discovery as we respond to his searching, probing, examining and prompting presence. It involves meeting ourselves as we really are, and recognising that God loves and accepts us, even if *we* don't. Yet there is another side to the coin, for that acceptance embraces not only us but others, all people important to him. On one level, the Samaritan woman's encounter with Jesus speaks of breaking down the barriers that separate us from God. On another, it speaks also of the barriers that separate us from one another.

Activity

The price is right (see page 68).

Reading: John 4:7, 9-11, 13-15

A woman of Samaria came to draw water, so Jesus asked her, 'Give me a drink.' The Samaritan woman responded, 'How can you, a Jew, ask me, a woman of Samaria, to give you a drink?' (Jews have no dealings with Samaritans.) Jesus answered her, 'If you knew the gift of God, and who has asked you, "Give me a drink", you would have made the request to him, and he would have given you living water.' The woman replied, 'Sir, the well is deep and you have no bucket, so where will you get this living water?' Jesus said to her, 'Anyone drinking the water here will thirst again, but whoever drinks the water I will give them will never be thirsty.' The woman said to him, 'Sir, give me this water, so that I need never thirst or come here again to draw water.'

Comment

Many of you will have watched *Antiques Roadshow*, a series that has enjoyed enduring popularity. Week in, week out, people bring an astonishing array of objects for the experts to cast an appraising eye over. An old painting hidden in the loft for years, an unusual ornament discovered in a junkshop, a piece of jewellery handed down as a family heirloom – all are brought forward for inspection, and surprisingly often turn out to be worth far more than in their owners' wildest dreams. Not, of course, that objects have to be of great financial value to be worth something to us. Financially they may be all but worthless yet still be of immeasurable sentimental value – a faded photograph, a dog-eared letter, a tacky souvenir may mean nothing to one but everything to another.

All this may seem a long way from the story of the woman by the well, yet there are parallels, for, as any discerning Jew reading her story would have spotted straightaway, here was someone who, by the yardstick of her time, displayed all the signs of a thoroughly worthless individual. First, she was a woman and thus treated automatically as an inferior, second, a Samaritan, and, third, she was living out of wedlock having previously been married an astonishing five times (Jewish law at the time permitted a maximum of two remarriages)! This was the sort of person no self-respecting individual would knowingly consort with; the sort God surely had no time for and whom others could thus legitimately dismiss in turn. If you think that sounds disturbing, more disturbing still is the fact that she probably saw herself in much the same way; the fact that she was there alone without anyone to chaperone her and willing to talk to Jesus was proof of how little she valued her reputation. Yet if she was happy to talk, she was also surprised at being approached: 'How can you, a Jew, ask me, a woman of Samaria, to give you a drink?' (John 4:9)

It was a fair question, for Jesus was flouting all the social rules and religious taboos, but that, of course, is precisely what he intended to do. His actions were as important as his words. Simply by talking to her, he was breaking the mould, challenging the prejudices of his day that kept people apart. Above all, he was telling this woman that she was worth something, a person in her own right, a unique individual with an equally unique place in God's purpose. Whatever anyone else thought, God had time for her, just as *he* did. Imagine how much that must have meant. Perhaps for the first time in years here was someone willing to give her a chance in life, ready to see beyond the outside to the person beneath. It wasn't that Jesus pretended she was perfect – far from it – but then she recognised her imperfections well enough anyway. Yet beneath everything that was wrong he saw someone who mattered, someone who God wanted to enjoy the happiness and fulfilment she must have despaired of ever finding.

Here is an incident with a powerful, radical thrust if we take it seriously, asking searching questions about the way we view both others and ourselves. It says first, how often do we undervalue people, imagining we can pass judgement on them based on the little we know of them? How often do we allow our own preconceptions or the prejudices of society to sway our opinion of others? How often do we pigeonhole people rather than respond to them as individuals? How often do we deem people acceptable or unacceptable according to how well they measure up to an arbitrary set of rules? Sadly, that is all too often the religious way, but it is not Christ's way. Throughout his ministry he identified with those discarded as worthless, assuring them that though society might throw them on the scrap heap, God never will.

Second, and by contrast, how often do we undervalue ourselves? Though we can sometimes be blind to our faults, we can also be our own hardest critic and harshest judge, condemning ourselves where others make allowances. Instead of seeing the good we see the bad, instead of recognising our strengths we dwell on our weaknesses, and so, deep down, despite the self-assured mask we wear for the world, we are consumed by a lack of self-worth, uncertain that anyone, least of all God, can really have time for us. Yet the message of the Samaritan woman and her meeting with Jesus is that we too matter, every one of us, God's love constantly reaching out to offer acceptance and new beginnings.

There is one further point, which in our fragmented world of today cannot be overstressed. The encounter at the heart of this story is not concerned simply with human worth in general, but, as with the book of Ruth that we looked at earlier, touches also upon religious intolerance. The woman was a Samaritan and Jesus a Jew, and for that reason alone, according to Jewish law, they should have had no dealings with each other. Simply by mixing with her, Jesus was making himself ceremonially unclean and thus, in many people's eyes, would have been putting himself beyond the pale. Yet here, as in his parables and ministry, Jesus emphasised that God cannot be contained by the walls we erect against one another. Yes, there are convictions we hold dear, truths we consider essential, principles we will not lightly surrender, but that does not mean they have to separate us from one another.

We are worth something to him, each one of us. You, the crowd you work with, the people you like, those you don't, the folk you approve of and those whose behaviour shocks you – all have a place in God's heart. Catholic, Protestant, liberal, fundamentalist, Christian, Muslim, Buddhist, Hindu – we all matter to God. Let that truth shape our lives, and so help to shape our world.

Summary

- What is worth nothing to some may be worth much to others.
- Measured by the Jewish law, the Samaritan woman would have been dismissed by many as worthless, yet Jesus defied convention by stopping to talk to her.
- Through conversing with the woman, Jesus showed that he valued her as a person, that in his and God's eyes she was worth something. Beneath her imperfections, he saw someone of infinite value.
- All too easily, prejudice and preconceptions can cause us to undervalue those around us.
- Equally, they can cause us to undervalue ourselves.
- Through his words and actions, Jesus particularly challenged the religious divides of his day. We need to recognise the common humanity that unites us beyond similar divisions today.

Discussion

- In what ways might we undervalue people? Can you recall experiences that have helped you to see another's true worth?
- What might cause us to undervalue ourselves? Does faith, for you, stress your worth or unworthiness?
- How far as Christians should we be ready to engage in dialogue with other faiths and be open to insights they may offer? Can Christianity enter into such dialogue yet remain true to itself?

Prayer

Living God,
　　we are guilty sometimes of devaluing both others and ourselves.
We see weaknesses and fail to consider strengths.
We dwell on failures and ignore success.
We look at the outside
　　instead of searching deeper beneath the surface.
Forgive us for overlooking our own potential
　　and closing our mind to that in those around us.
Forgive us for finding it so easy to put people down
　　and so hard to build them up.
Teach us to recognise that everyone has a place in your purpose
　　and a contribution to make to your kingdom,
　　and so help us to see beyond the barriers that keep us apart
　　to everything that draws us together,
　　through Jesus Christ our Lord.
Amen.

Meditation of the woman of Samaria

He was full of surprises, that man,
　　from the moment I first met him.
I thought he'd just push me aside like all the rest;
　　either that or walk away with his head in the air.
He was a Jew, remember, and I a Samaritan;
　　and, worse than that,
　　a woman,
　　alone.
Yet he stayed where he was, a smile on his face,
　　quite happy, apparently, to be associated with me.
Well, call me suspicious, if you like,
　　but I wasn't sure what he was up to,
So I asked him straight out, 'What's your game?'
He laughed at that, and then offered me a drink of water –

at least I thought that's what he was doing,
though I wasn't sure.
You see, he had no bucket,
and he could hardly shin down the well, could he?
So where was this water he was on about meant to come from?
To be frank, I suspected he was pulling my leg,
but I was beginning to like him despite the nonsense he talked.
He had a nice way with him,
kind,
gentle,
a bit of all right in an unconventional sort of way.
So I played along, wondering where it would all lead.
If only I'd known,
what an embarrassment I might have saved myself.
I'll never know how he guessed,
but suddenly he looked straight at me
and for the first time I noticed his eyes.
They didn't undress you like so many men's seem to do,
but looked much deeper,
almost as if into my very soul,
and then he started talking about my lovers,
my husbands,
my past –
every detail correct.
It was uncanny,
frightening,
far too near the knuckle,
so I tried to fob him off with some old chestnut about worship.
But even then he threw me;
none of the usual pat answers
but a response that reached right to the heart of the matter,
cutting through all the trivia.
And it was after that he produced the biggest surprise of all –
told me he was the Messiah!
I didn't know what to say,
just stood there gawping, flabbergasted.

I mean, I realised he was a prophet,
    but the Messiah?
It couldn't be, I told myself,
    no way.
I went back down to the village, seeking reassurance,
    wanting someone to tell me he was just another religious nutcase.
But they didn't.
They were curious,
    wanted to see for themselves.
And when they heard him,
    listened to his teaching,
    they believed he was the Messiah.
Me? I still don't know, but I'll tell you this,
    whatever I believe about him,
    he seemed somehow to believe in me!

Further reading: Psalm 139:23-24

Search me, O God, and know my heart; test me and know my thoughts. See if there is any misguided way in me, and lead me in your eternal path.

Suggestions for action

Focus this week on your strengths rather than your weaknesses. Do the same with those around you. Look for the good rather than the bad.

Closing prayer

Lord Jesus Christ,
    open my heart to your searching presence,
    and teach me to respond to your challenging word,
    however unsettling that might be.
Amen.

Sixth week

Lydia: Voice of commitment

Opening prayer

Lord, whose way is perfect,
  help me always to trust in your goodness,
  that walking with you
  and following you in all simplicity,
  I may possess a quiet and contented mind
  and may cast all care on you,
  for you care for me.
Amen.

Christina Rossetti

Introduction

In some ways, the story of Lydia is similar to that of Esther, in that both women made a distinctive stand, putting their security on the line for others. The difference is that Esther saw her action as primarily one of solidarity with her people, while Lydia saw hers as an expression of solidarity with Christ. There is another difference. Lydia had reached where she was, not _because_ of her sex but _despite_ it. She was, if you like, a self-made woman, and, as such, with the exception of Martha, her story has less to say about prejudice than those we have explored thus far. Yet it still lurks beneath the surface, even if in a sense we may not usually associate with the term. We live today in a post-Christian society, notwithstanding the fact that most people claim some kind of Christian faith. The majority are not hostile to the claims of Christ but indifferent, and as for the Church, it is dismissed as irrelevant, out-of-date and slightly odd. We are unlikely to face persecution or be discriminated against for following Jesus, yet it is not always easy to profess the name of Christ. None of us likes to be thought different, still less as strange. It couldn't have been any easier for Lydia though; whatever we have to lose she probably had far more. Her simple story affords a continuing challenge to each of us today.

Activity
Quiz (see page 69).

Reading: Acts 16:13-15
On the sabbath day we went outside the gate by the river, where we supposed there was a place of prayer; and we sat down and spoke to the women who had gathered there. A certain woman named Lydia, a worshipper of God, was listening to us; she was from the city of Thyatira and a dealer in purple cloth. The Lord opened her heart to listen eagerly to what was said by Paul. When she and her household were baptised, she urged us, saying, 'If you have judged me to be faithful to the Lord, come and stay at my home.' And she prevailed upon us. (*NRSV*)

Comment
Imagine picking up your newspaper tomorrow and reading that your favourite supermarket was involved in a major worldwide scandal. Would you continue to shop there? It's possible you still would, if only because you have no viable alternative, but it's equally possible that you would go elsewhere, even if it meant putting yourself out. There are few things big business fears more than a bad press. The old adage may claim that all publicity is good publicity, but experiences have shown otherwise. It only

takes a hint of scandal, a suggestion of malpractice, to send a firm's profits tumbling and slash the price of its shares.

All this may seem a long way from the woman we're considering in the last of our series, for Lydia could hardly be described as big business, let alone discussed in the same breath as today's multinational corporations, yet the analogy is nonetheless worth pursuing. In the context of her time, she was a woman of substance who had achieved financial success through building up what must have been a thriving and lucrative business. How can we be so sure? The answer is there in one small but vital detail, for it wasn't just *any* cloth she dealt in but *purple* cloth – in other words, the imperial colour of Rome worn only by the emperor and those of rank and authority. Lydia's, then, was clearly no run-of-the-mill business but one that dealt in exclusive, top-of-the-range goods. Establishing such an enterprise represents no mean feat. To not only hold her own but also prosper in the cut-throat world of commerce, Lydia must have been someone with her head screwed on, a woman of shrewd business acumen. She would have understood as well as any the importance of keeping in with the right people, avoiding anything that might damage her reputation or in any way deter clients. One careless move, one unwise decision, could have costly consequences. Yet a chance encounter by the riverside was to lead her to put at risk everything she had worked so hard to build up. One moment, she had been gathering with her friends to worship God, as was her custom; the next, she had declared her faith in Christ, a man she had never known or seen, and invited his followers into her home. 'The Lord opened her heart to listen eagerly to what was said by Paul. When she and her household were baptised, she urged us, saying, "If you have judged me to be faithful to the Lord, come and stay at my home." And she prevailed upon us' (Acts 16:14b-15, *NRSV*).

What, you may ask, was so dangerous about that? Why should her decision to follow Christ have any bearing upon the future of her business? Surely the two matters were completely different? Had we been talking of today, that might have been true, but *then* it was a different matter. Judaism – the religion Lydia followed –

had become accepted, but Christianity was another matter, in many parts of the Roman Empire arousing suspicion and hatred, frequently fomented by the Jews themselves. Even in these early days, Christians found themselves under the cosh, their beliefs misunderstood, their customs distorted and their name used as a scapegoat for all kinds of trouble.

It is not hard to imagine what her friends must have said and how appalled they must have been. What was she thinking of, getting mixed up in this newfangled religion? Had she thought through the implications of her decision? Had she any idea what it all might cost? And, of course, it's just possible that she hadn't. After all, this was the first time Paul had visited Philippi and, as far as we know, the first time the gospel was preached in this part of the world. Maybe she made her initial commitment in all innocence, oblivious to the controversy surrounding Christianity or the official Jewish line towards it. Perhaps when she learned more about it, she might yet change her mind and avoid damaging her prospects.

If any thought that, they were in for a disappointment, for Lydia was soon to be left under no illusions as to the cost of serving Jesus. An incident in the marketplace in which Paul challenged the exploitation of a young and disturbed slave girl led to him and Silas both being set upon by the mob, accused of treason and flung into jail, and though they were later released the die had been cast, no question now as to the sort of response Christians could expect. As a market-trader herself, getting involved with this man spelt trouble with a capital 'T'; as a supplier of cloth to the authorities, it meant alienating her most valued customers; as a Jew, it meant estranging herself from those with whom she'd worshipped; as a citizen of Philippi, it risked making herself a social leper. Yet she carried on regardless. Why? Not because of Paul, but because of Jesus Christ, the one he proclaimed and in whose name he acted. Instead of disassociating herself as quickly as possible from everything to do with Paul, and instead of reconsidering her decision to follow Christ, she opened her home to those who had come to faith, and, as Acts 16:40 tells us, on their release from prison she welcomed Paul and Silas as well. For all we know, it may be that the church in Philippi to which Paul wrote one of his letters continued to meet at that time in her home!

A woman proud to be associated with the name of Christ; like Paul himself, not ashamed of the gospel or concerned at the prospect of misunderstanding, rejection and hostility arising from her decision to follow Christ. Here was a woman who was prepared to put her faith before all else, even if it meant risking everything she had worked so hard to achieve. Her lesson for us today is straightforward enough. How ready are we to be identified with Christ, to stand up and stand out for him even when it may be costly or demanding to do so? How willing are we to put Christ first, even when it may clash with other interests? How far do we make our faith public rather than keep it a private affair between God and ourselves? How much are we ready to sacrifice, should it be asked of us? In Lydia we see a woman prepared to risk everything for one who had given everything for her. Have we the faith and commitment to follow her example?

Summary

- Anyone in business will know how damaging bad publicity can be, but Lydia willingly identified herself with a new and controversial religion.

- If she was under any illusions as to the damage being associated with Christianity could cause, these were surely dispelled by the arrest and imprisonment of Paul and Silas. Yet she not only entertained Christians in her home but also welcomed back Paul and Silas following their release from prison.

- Through continuing to follow Christ, Lydia put at risk her relationships with her Jewish friends, fellow dealers, clients and townspeople. She clearly believed that in him she had found someone who made the possible sacrifices involved more than worth it.

- How far are we upfront about our Christian commitment? Are we ready, as Lydia was, to put Jesus first and ourselves second?

61

Discussion

- In what ways today might discipleship clash with other interests? What sacrifices might we as Christians be called to make?

- Are there times when we feel tempted to keep quiet about our faith? Why? Might this ever be justified?

- Are there those we know of who have stood out for their faith, even when it prejudiced their prospects or led to them being the object of ridicule? Were they right to make such a stand?

Prayer

Lord Jesus Christ,
    you identified yourself totally with humankind,
    sharing not just our life but our death.
Forgive us that sometimes we are reluctant to be identified with you.
We are afraid of what people may think,
    embarrassed by the possibility of being misunderstood,
    worried that it may affect our prospects,
    nervous about what it might lead to.
Lord Jesus,
    help us to put you first in our lives,
    even when that might mean putting other things we value second.
Teach us to show in our lives what we claim to be true with our lips.
Amen.

Meditation of Lydia

They all think I'm mad, getting mixed up in this Jesus business –
    ought to have more sense they say –
    and I can understand their reasons well enough.
You see, I'd have thought the same once.
Why take any chances when you've worked so hard

to make a success of your life?
Why risk everything for the sake of some newfangled religion?
Yet let's be fair, I'd already put myself out on a limb,
    rejecting the idols of Rome to worship the God of Israel.
That was bordering on the eccentric,
    more than a trifle suspect in some people's eyes.
Yet while it may have made me different,
    even perhaps considered a little odd,
    it hadn't actually harmed my prospects.
A matter of choice, that was the way people saw it;
    they go their way and I mine.
So I did just that.
And though I say it myself, I made a good fist of it –
    my business thriving,
    my lifestyle more than comfortable,
    myself respected,
    a valued member of the community,
    successful pillar of the establishment.
But then I heard about Jesus, and I was fascinated immediately.
I suppose it was the way Paul spoke of him.
His faith was so real,
    so alive,
    almost radiating from him,
    and I listened entranced to everything he had to say,
    knowing that this man Jesus was for me,
    the one thing missing in my life,
    the answer I'd long been looking for.
What else could I do but accept him?
How else respond than declare him as Lord?
Yes, I knew the controversy surrounding him,
    the hatred of the Jews,
    suspicion of the Romans,
    and I understood from the beginning it might be costly,
    possibly risking everything I'd worked for,
    maybe even more.
Once I'd opened my home like that,

welcomed his followers,
offered hospitality,
there could be no going back.
I'd shown my colours,
made my stand,
identified myself with Jesus beyond question.
So yes, perhaps I am mad,
perhaps I ought to think again,
but it makes no difference.
Though they urge me to keep quiet,
implore me not to make a show,
I have no choice –
I *have* to follow, serve him, play my part, come what may.
Oh, I know they mean well,
that they want to save me from myself,
and I'm touched by their concern, believe me.
But even if they're right and I do end up losing everything,
it doesn't matter,
for I've found far, far more
than anything I may ever have to sacrifice.

Further reading: Romans 1:16

I am not ashamed of the gospel, for it is God's power bringing
salvation to all who believe, to the Jew first and to the Gentile.

Suggestions for action

If you've bitten your tongue sometimes concerning your faith,
playing it down or even concealing it altogether, make a point of
being honest and open about it.

Closing prayer

Living God,
   you gave yourself wholly to us in Christ,
   glad to call us your children.
Teach us to give ourselves similarly to you,
   proud to call you our Father
   and happy to be identified with your Son.
In his name we ask it.
Amen.

Appendix 1
Activities

First week: Ruth

Quiz

The following have either worked for the cause of the outsider, or experienced being an outsider themselves.

1. Nineteenth-century nurse, hospital reformer and humanitarian
2. Supplied humanitarian relief during the American Civil War and founded the American Red Cross
3. Celebrated by many as a twentieth-century saint for her work among the poor
4. Young girl executed at Belsen concentration camp, whose legacy has touched the hearts of millions
5. English writer whose novels explored female sexuality in a male-dominated world
6. A suffragette who threw herself under the king's horse in 1913
7. An Australian who campaigned over many years for a proper representation of women
8. Campaigned in America for social reform, women's suffrage, worker's rights and First World War detainees

Second week: Esther

Quiz

Match the following women to the correct date for their respective achievements.

1. Virginia Wade (Wimbledon champion)
2. Margaret Thatcher (first woman Prime Minister)

3. Betty Boothroyd (first woman speaker of House of Commons)
4. Spice Girls (their first number one hit)
5. J. K. Rowling (first Harry Potter book published)
6. Valentina Tereshkova (first woman in space)
7. First Anglican women priests
8. Ellen MacArthur (fastest woman to sail round the world)

1992
1996
1977
2001
1997
1994
1979
1963

Afterwards, talk briefly about being in the right place at the right time, and what it takes to grasp a moment of opportunity.

Third week: Mary, sister of Martha
Screwball Scramble®
Play the game Screwball Scramble®, Race against Time, or any other game you can think of that involves racing against the clock. Discuss afterwards people's feelings as time ticks by, and consider how often and in what ways we experience such feelings during daily life.

Fourth week: The woman who touched Jesus' cloak
Quiz
The following all refused to give up the pursuit of their cause, despite the obstacles they faced.

1. Forceful opponent of slavery, as seen in her celebrated book *Uncle Tom's Cabin*
2. A nurse in occupied Europe during the Second World War, she went on to establish homes for sick and disabled people across the world
3. An itinerant preacher, opponent of slavery and advocate of women's rights
4. Celebrated US social reformer who led the struggle for women's rights
5. Dedicated her life to the work of prison reform
6. The first woman doctor and, later, first woman mayor in England
7. Made a Dame for her work in the suffrage movement and for her campaign to secure higher education for women
8. British suffrage leader, frequently imprisoned for her militant campaign to secure the right to vote for women

Afterwards, talk together briefly about the qualities needed not to give up despite setbacks.

Fifth week: The woman of Samaria

The price is right

Prepare your own version of the television show, inviting group members to guess the price of various everyday items (for example, a packet of tea, bag of sugar, bar of chocolate; you can use pictures of these, or simply print the name of each, if you don't want to buy them). You could either select a panel from among the group, leaving remaining members as the 'audience', or ask all group members to have a guess. You can suggest three prices for people to choose from, or leave it to participants to make their own guess. Afterwards, talk briefly about how we put a price on something, and consider in what ways we attach worth or otherwise to people.

Sixth week: Lydia

Quiz

The following all put their own safety at risk because of their convictions.

1. A nurse executed by the Gestapo following her shielding of British, French and Belgian soldiers in her home
2. Legendary figure involved in politics and social welfare in Argentina before a military crackdown
3. Revered by many as a saint, she was burned to death for her faith
4. Marine biologist who became an ecological campaigner; author of *Silent Spring*
5. Stateswoman who, as leader of the Pakistan People's Party campaigned for open elections in that country
6. First woman Prime Minister of Israel, she hoped to secure peace in the Middle East through diplomatic means
7. Indian Prime Minister who worked as a leader of developing nations until her assassination in 1984
8. Became President of the Republic of the Philippines, following her opposition to the corrupt Marcos regime

Afterwards, talk briefly together about the beliefs or people members of the group would be willing to make sacrifices for.

Appendix 2

Answers

First week: Ruth
1. Florence Nightingale
2. Clara Barton
3. Mother Teresa
4. Anne Frank
5. Fay Weldon
6. Emily Davison
7. Germaine Greer
8. Elizabeth Gurley Smith

Second week: Esther
1. Virginia Wade (Wimbledon champion) 1977
2. Margaret Thatcher (first woman Prime Minister) 1979
3. Betty Boothroyd (first woman speaker of House of Commons) 1992
4. Spice Girls (their first number one hit) 1996
5. J. K. Rowling (first Harry Potter book) 1997
6. Valentina Tereshkova (first woman in space) 1963
7. First Anglican women priests 1994
8. Ellen MacArthur (fastest woman to sail round the world) 2001

Fourth week: The woman who touched Jesus' cloak

1. Harriet Beecher Stowe
2. Sue Ryder
3. Sojourner Truth
4. Elizabeth Cady Stanton
5. Elizabeth Fry
6. Elizabeth Garrett Anderson
7. Dame Millicent Fawcett
8. Emmeline Pankhurst

Sixth week: Lydia

1. Edith Cavell
2. Eva Perón
3. Joan of Arc
4. Rachel Carson
5. Benazir Bhutto
6. Golda Meir
7. Indira Gandhi
8. Corazon Aquino

Also in this series:
Living with questions – exploring faith and doubt
Paul – the man and the mission
Something to share – communicating the good news
Prayer – the fundamental questions
Unsung gifts – the Spirit at work in the New Testament
Discipleship – the journey of faith
Love – the key to it all

Also by Nick Fawcett:
No ordinary man (books 1 and 2)
Resources for reflective worship on the person of Jesus

The unfolding story
Resources for reflective worship on the Old Testament

Grappling with God (books 1-4)
Old Testament studies for personal and small-group use

To put it another way
Resources for reflective worship on the Parables

Are you listening?
Honest prayers about life

Prayers for all seasons (books 1 and 2)
A comprehensive resource for public worship

Getting it across
One hundred talks for family worship

Decisions, decisions
A Lent study course

Promises, promises
An Advent study course

Daily prayer
A book of daily devotions

All the above titles are available from your local Christian bookshop
or direct from Kevin Mayhew Ltd, telephone 01449 737978,
fax: 01449 737834, email: sales@kevinmayhewltd.com